STEP-BY-STEP

Italian Regional Cooking

Italian Regional Cooking

ROSEMARY WADEY

||| •PARRAGON• |||

First published in Great Britain in 1994 by
Parragon Book Service Ltd
Unit 13–17
Avonbridge Trading Estate
Atlantic Road
Avonmouth
Bristol BS11 9QD

ISBN 1-85813-614-8 (hbk)
ISBN 0-75251-272-2 (pbk)

Printed in Italy

Acknowledgements:
Design & DTP: Pedro & Frances Prá-Lopez/Kingfisher Design
Art Direction: Clive Hayball
Managing Editor: Alexa Stace
Special Photography: Martin Brigdale
Home Economist: Jill Eggleton
Cover Photography: Clive Streeter
Step-by-step Photography: Karl Adamson
Step-by-step Home Economist: Joanna Craig
Styling: Helen Trent

Photographs on pages 6, 22, 38, 48 and 62 reproduced by permission of
ZEFA Picture Library UK Ltd.

Note:
*Cup measurements in this book are for American cups. Tablespoons are assumed to be 15 ml.
Unless otherwise stated, milk is assumed to be full-fat, eggs are standard size 2 and pepper is freshly
ground black pepper.*

Contents

Antipasto & Soups

The word antipasto means "before the main course" and what is served may be simple and inexpensive or highly elaborate. Antipasto usually comes in three categories: meat, fish and vegetables. There are many varieties of cold meats, including ham, invariably sliced paper-thin. The best known is Parma ham, but there are many others, especially from the mountain areas, all of which can be served with slices of melon and figs. Numerous vegetables feature in antipasto dishes, served raw or marinated, deep-fried or pickled, with and without dressings. All varieties of fish are combined for the antipasto di pesce, often depending on availability but including inkfish, octopus and cuttlefish. Huge prawns (shrimp) and mussels appear in various guises and fresh sardines are always popular.

Soups too are a very important part of the Italian cuisine. They vary in consistency from very thin to virtually knife and fork soups. Minestrone is known world-wide but the best-known version probably came from Milan; however, all varieties are full of vegetables, often with pasta or rice plus beans, and are delicious and satisfying. Fish soups abound in one guise or another, and most of these are village specialities, so the variety is unlimited. Many of these soups constitute a whole meal, particularly those with a large proportion of beans, or with lightly toasted slices of bread added to the bowl.

Opposite: *The Grand Canal, Venice. With its close proximity to the sea, fish and seafood dishes are found in abundance around Venice and the north-east corner of Italy.*

FISH SOUP

*All over Italy the selection of fish is enormous. There are many varieties
of fish soup, some including shellfish. You will find cream soups, thin
soups and thick soups: this one, from Tuscany, is more like a chowder.*

STEP 1a

STEP 1b

STEP 4

STEP 5

SERVES 4-6

1 kg/2 lb assorted prepared fish (including
   mixed fish fillets, squid etc)
2 onions, peeled and thinly sliced
a few sprigs of parsley
2 bay leaves
2 celery sticks, thinly sliced
150 ml/¼ pint/⅔ cup white wine
1 litre/1¾ pints/4 cups water
2 tbsp olive oil
1 garlic clove, crushed
1 carrot, peeled and finely chopped
1 x 425 g/15 oz can peeled tomatoes,
   puréed
2 potatoes, peeled and chopped
1 tbsp tomato purée (paste)
1 tsp freshly chopped oregano or ½ tsp
   dried oregano
350 g/12 oz fresh mussels
175 g/6 oz peeled prawns (shrimp)
2 tbsp freshly chopped parsley
salt and pepper
crusty bread, to serve

1 Cut the cleaned and prepared fish
into slices or cubes and put into a
large saucepan with 1 sliced onion, the
parsley sprigs and bay leaves, 1 sliced
celery stick, the wine and the water.
Bring to the boil, cover and simmer for
about 25 minutes.

2 Strain the fish stock and discard the
vegetables. Skin the fish, remove
any bones and reserve.

3 Heat the oil in a pan, finely chop
the remaining onion and fry with
the garlic, remaining celery and carrot
until soft but not coloured. Add the
puréed canned tomatoes, potatoes,
tomato purée (paste), oregano, reserved
stock and seasonings. Bring to the boil
and simmer for about 15 minutes or
until the potato is almost tender.

4 Meanwhile, thoroughly scrub the
mussels. Add to the pan with the
prawns (shrimp) and simmer for about 5
minutes or until the mussels have opened
(discard any that stay closed).

5 Return the fish to the soup with the
chopped parsley, bring back to the
boil and simmer for 5 minutes. Adjust
the seasoning.

6 Serve the soup in warmed bowls
with chunks of fresh crusty bread,
or put a toasted slice of crusty bread in
the bottom of each bowl before adding
the soup. If possible, remove a few half
shells from the mussels before serving.

RED BEAN SOUP

*Beans feature widely in Italian soups, making them hearty and tasty.
You can use other varieties of beans in this soup
(from Tuscany and Lazio), if preferred.*

STEP 1

STEP 2

STEP 4

STEP 5

SERVES 4-6

*175 g/6 oz/scant 1 cup dried red kidney
    beans, soaked overnight
1.7 litres/3 pints/7¹/₂ cups water
1 large ham bone or bacon knuckle
2 carrots, peeled and chopped
1 large onion, peeled and chopped
2 celery sticks, thinly sliced
1 leek, trimmed, washed and sliced
1-2 bay leaves
2 tbsp olive oil
2-3 tomatoes, peeled and chopped
1 garlic clove, crushed
1 tbsp tomato purée (paste)
60 g/2 oz/4 tbsp arborio or Italian rice
125-175 g/4-6 oz green cabbage, finely
    shredded
salt and pepper*

1 Drain the beans and put into a
saucepan with enough water to
cover. Bring to the boil and boil hard for
15 minutes, then reduce the heat and
simmer for 45 minutes. The hard boiling
is essential with red beans for safety
reasons. Drain.

2 Put the beans into a clean
saucepan with the measured
amount of water, ham bone or knuckle,
carrots, onion, celery, leek, bay leaves
and olive oil. Bring to the boil, cover and
simmer for an hour or until the beans are
very tender.

3 Discard the bay leaves and bone,
reserving any ham pieces from the
bone. Remove a small cupful of the beans
and reserve. Purée or liquidize the soup
in a food processor or blender and return
to a clean pan.

4 Add the tomatoes, garlic, tomato
purée (paste), rice and plenty of
seasoning, bring back to the boil and
simmer for about 15 minutes or until the
rice is tender.

5 Add the cabbage and reserved
beans and ham and continue to
simmer for 5 minutes. Adjust the
seasoning and serve very hot. If liked, a
piece of toasted crusty bread may be put
in the base of each soup bowl before
ladling in the soup. If the soup is too
thick, add a little boiling water or stock.

MINESTRONE WITH PESTO

*One of the many versions of minestrone, which is always full of a
variety of vegetables, pasta and rice and often includes beans. This soup
is flavoured with pesto sauce, so often added to pasta dishes.*

STEP 1

SERVES 6

*175 g/6 oz/scant 1 cup dried cannellini
    beans, soaked overnight*
2.5 litres/4 pints/10 cups water or stock
1 large onion, peeled and chopped
1 leek, trimmed and thinly sliced
2 celery stalks, very thinly sliced
2 carrots, peeled and chopped
3 tbsp olive oil
2 tomatoes, peeled and roughly chopped
*1 courgette (zucchini), trimmed and thinly
    sliced*
2 potatoes, peeled and diced
*90 g/3 oz elbow macaroni (or other small
    macaroni)*
salt and pepper
4-6 tbsp Parmesan, grated

PESTO:
2 tbsp pine kernels
5 tbsp olive oil
2 bunches fresh basil, stems removed
4-6 garlic cloves, crushed
*90 g /3 oz/³/4 cup Pecorino or Parmesan,
    grated*
salt and pepper

1 Drain the beans, rinse and place in
a saucepan with the measured
water or stock. Bring to the boil, cover
and simmer gently for 1 hour.

2 Add the onion, leek, celery, carrots,
and oil. Cover and simmer for 4-5
minutes.

3 Add the tomatoes, courgette
(zucchini), potatoes and macaroni
and seasoning, cover again and continue
to simmer for about 30 minutes or until
very tender.

4 Meanwhile, make the pesto. Fry
the pine kernels in 1 tablespoon of
the oil until pale brown, then drain. Put
the basil into a food processor or blender
with the nuts and garlic. Process until
well chopped. Gradually add the oil until
smooth. Turn into a bowl, add the cheese
and seasoning and mix thoroughly.

5 Stir 1½ tablespoons of the pesto into
the soup until well blended,
simmer for a further 5 minutes and
adjust the seasoning. Serve very hot,
sprinkled with the cheese.

STEP 2

STEP 3

PESTO

Store in an airtight container for up to a
week in the refrigerator; or freeze (without
adding the cheese) for several months.

STEP 5

STEP 2

STEP 3

STEP 4

STEP 5

AUBERGINE (EGGPLANT) SALAD

*A starter with a difference from Sicily. It has a real bite, both from the
sweet-sour sauce, with its surprising flavouring of chocolate,
and from the texture of the celery.*

SERVES 4

*2 large aubergines (eggplant), about 1 kg/
    2 lb
salt
6 tbsp olive oil
1 small onion, peeled and finely chopped
2 garlic cloves, crushed
6-8 celery sticks
2 tbsp capers
12-16 green olives, pitted and sliced
2 tbsp pine kernels
30 g/ 1 oz bitter or plain chocolate, grated
4 tbsp wine vinegar
1 tbsp brown sugar
salt and pepper
2 hard-boiled eggs, sliced, to serve
celery leaves or curly endive, to garnish*

1 Cut the aubergines (eggplant) into
2.5 cm/1 in cubes and sprinkle
liberally with 2-3 tablespoons salt. Leave
to stand for an hour, to extract the bitter
juices, then rinse off the salt thoroughly
under cold water, drain and dry on paper
towels.

2 Heat most of the oil in a frying pan
and fry the aubergines (eggplant)
cubes until golden brown all over. Drain
on paper towels then transfer them to a
large bowl.

3 Add the onion and garlic to the pan
with the remaining oil and fry very
gently until just soft. Cut the celery into
1 cm/½ in slices, add to the pan and fry
for a few minutes, stirring frequently,
until lightly coloured but still crisp.

4 Add the celery to the aubergines
(eggplant) with the capers, olives
and pine kernels and mix lightly.

5 Add the chocolate and vinegar to
the residue in the pan with the
sugar. Heat gently until melted, then
bring up to the boil. Season with a little
salt and plenty of freshly ground black
pepper and pour over the salad. Mix
lightly, cover, leave until cold and then
chill thoroughly.

6 Serve with sliced hard-boiled eggs
and garnish with celery leaves or
curly endive.

NOTE

This salad will keep for several days in a
covered container in the refrigerator.
Chopped green tomatoes may also be
added to this salad, in season.

MOZZARELLA IN CAROZZA

*A delicious way of serving cheese, a speciality of Campania and the
Abruzzi. The cheese stretches out into melted strings as you
cut it to eat. Some versions have Parma ham added, too.*

STEP 1

SERVES 4

200 g/ 7 oz Mozzarella
4 slices, about 90 g/ 3 oz, Parma ham
*8 slices white bread, preferably 2 days old,
   crusts removed*
a little butter for spreading
2 - 3 eggs
3 tbsp milk
vegetable oil, for deep frying
salt and pepper

TOMATO AND PEPPER SAUCE:
1 onion, peeled and chopped
2 garlic cloves, crushed
3 tbsp olive oil
*1 red (bell) pepper, cored, seeded and
   chopped*
1 x 425 g/ 15 oz can peeled tomatoes
2 tbsp tomato purée (paste)
3 tbsp water
1 tbsp lemon juice
flat-leaf parsley, to garnish (optional)

1 First make the sauce: fry the onion
and garlic in the oil until soft. Add
the (bell) pepper and continue to cook for
a few minutes. Add the tomatoes, tomato
purée (paste), water, lemon juice and
seasoning, bring up to the boil, cover and
simmer for 10-15 minutes or until
tender. Cool the sauce a little then purée

or liquidize until smooth and return to a
clean pan.

2 Cut the Mozzarella into 4 slices so
they are as large as possible; if a
square piece of cheese cut into 8 slices.
Trim the Parma ham slices to the same
size as the cheese.

3 Lightly butter the bread and use
the cheese and ham to make 4
sandwiches, pressing the edges well
together. If liked they may be cut in half
at this stage. Chill.

STEP 3

4 Lightly beat the eggs with the milk
and seasoning in a shallow dish.

5 Carefully dip the sandwiches in the
egg mixture until well coated all
over, and if possible leave to soak for a
few minutes.

STEP 5

6 Heat the oil in a large pan or deep-
frier until it just begins to smoke, or
until a cube of bread browns in about 30
seconds. Fry the sandwiches in batches
until golden brown on both sides. Drain
well on crumpled paper towels and keep
warm. Serve the sandwiches hot, with
the reheated tomato and pepper sauce,
and garnished with parsley.

STEP 6

CROSTINI ALLA FIORENTINA

A coarse pâté from Tuscany which can be served as a starter or simply spread on small pieces of crusty fried bread (crostini) to serve as an appetizer with drinks.

STEP 1

STEP 2

STEP 3

STEP 6

SERVES 4

3 tbsp olive oil
1 onion, peeled and chopped
1 celery stick, chopped
1 carrot, peeled and chopped
1-2 garlic cloves, crushed
125 g/4 oz chicken livers
125 g/4 oz calf's, lamb's or pig's liver
150 ml/¼ pint/⅔ cup red wine
1 tbsp tomato purée (paste)
2 tbsp freshly chopped parsley
3-4 canned anchovy fillets, finely chopped
2 tbsp stock or water
30-45 g/1-1½ oz/2-3 tbsp butter
1 tbsp capers
salt and pepper
small pieces of fried crusty bread (see right)
chopped parsley, to garnish

1 Heat the oil in a pan, add the onion, celery, carrot and garlic and cook gently for 4-5 minutes or until the onion is soft, but not coloured.

2 Meanwhile, rinse and dry the chicken livers. Dry the calf's or other liver, and slice into strips. Add the liver to the pan and fry gently for a few minutes until the strips are well sealed on all sides.

3 Add half the wine and cook until mostly evaporated then add the rest of the wine, tomato purée (paste), half the parsley, anchovy fillets, stock or water, a little salt and plenty of black pepper.

4 Cover the pan and simmer for 15-20 minutes or until tender and most of the liquid has been absorbed.

5 Cool the mixture a little then either coarsely mince or put into a food processor and process until coarsely blended.

6 Return to the pan and add the butter, remaining parsley and capers and heat through gently until the butter melts. Adjust the seasoning and turn into a bowl. Serve warm or cold spread on the slices of crusty bread and sprinkled with chopped parsley.

CROSTINI

To make crostini, slice a crusty loaf or a French loaf into small rounds or squares. Heat olive oil in a frying pan and fry the slices until golden brown and crisp. Drain on paper towels.

STEP 1

SEAFOOD SALAD

Fresh seafood is plentiful in Italy and varieties of seafood salads are found all over the regions. Each has its own speciality, depending on availability and what appears in each day's catch.

SERVES 4

175 g/6 oz squid rings, defrosted if frozen
600 ml/1 pint/2½ cups water
150 ml/¼ pint/⅔ cup dry white wine
250 g/8 oz hake or monkfish, cut into cubes
16-20 fresh mussels, scrubbed and beards removed
20 clams in shells, scrubbed, if available (otherwise use extra mussels)
125-175 g/4-6 oz peeled prawns (shrimp)
3-4 spring onions (scallions) trimmed and sliced (optional)
radicchio and curly endive leaves, to serve
lemon wedges, to garnish

DRESSING
6 tbls olive oil
1 tbls wine vinegar
2 tbls freshly chopped parsley
1-2 garlic cloves, crushed
salt and pepper

GARLIC MAYONNAISE
5 tbls thick mayonnaise
2-3 tbls fromage frais or natural yogurt
2 garlic cloves, crushed
1 tbls capers
2 tbls freshly chopped parsley or mixed herbs

1 Poach the squid in the water and wine for 20 minutes or until nearly tender. Add the fish cubes and continue to cook gently for 7-8 minutes or until tender. Strain, reserving the fish, and place the stock in a clean pan.

2 Bring the fish stock to the boil and add the mussels and clams. Cover the pan and simmer gently for about 5 minutes or until the shells open. Discard any that stay closed.

3 Drain the shellfish and remove from their shells. Put into a bowl with the cooked fish and add the prawns (shrimp) and onions (scallions) if using.

4 For the dressing, whisk together the oil, vinegar, parsley, garlic, salt and plenty of black pepper. Pour over the fish, mix well, cover and chill for several hours.

5 Arrange small leaves of radicchio and curly endive on 4 plates and spoon the fish salad into the centre. Garnish each plate with lemon wedges. Combine all the ingredients for the garlic mayonnaise and serve with the salad.

STEP 2

STEP 3

STEP 4

Pasta & Pizza

It is well known that Italians are prolific eaters of pasta, but it may not be realized just how many varieties of pasta there are; in fact it runs to many hundreds, and it would be almost impossible to list them all. Home-made pasta only takes a few minutes to cook while the bought variety takes longer, and it is best to follow the cooking directions on the pack. If you are going to make a lot of pasta it is well worth investing in a pasta-making machine, which will enable you to produce quantities with the minimum of effort. Pasta is of Genoese origin but nowadays is even more popular in Naples and the southern regions of Italy; while in the north of the country a fair amount of rice is consumed. Milanese and other risottos are made with short-grain Italian rice, the best of which is Arborio, but remember that this type of rice should never be rinsed before cooking. An Italian risotto is far moister than a pilau or other savoury rice, but it should not be soggy or sticky.

Gnocchi are made from maize flour, cornmeal (polenta), potatoes or semolina, often combined with spinach and some sort of cheese. They resemble dumplings, and are either poached or baked, and served with some variety of cheese sauce. Polenta is made with either cornmeal or polenta flour and can be served either as a soft porridge or hard cake which is then fried. The traditional method of making polenta involved long slow cooking, but now there is an excellent polenta mix available which cuts the time to 5 minutes!

Opposite: The market in the Piazza della Fratta, Padua, offers a wide selection of fruit and vegetables. Italians like to shop daily, to make sure their produce is absolutely fresh.

STEP 2

STEP 3a

STEP 3b

STEP 4

TORTELLINI

According to legend the shape of the tortellini is said to resemble the tummy button of Venus, but suffice to say that when you make tortellini from this description you know exactly what they should look like!

SERVES 4

FILLING
125 g/4 oz boneless, skinned chicken breast
60 g/2 oz prosciutto or Parma ham
45 g/1½ oz cooked spinach, well drained
1 tbsp finely chopped onion
2 tbsp grated Parmesan
good pinch of ground allspice
1 egg, beaten
salt and pepper
1 quantity Pasta Dough (see page 76)

SAUCE:
300 ml/½ pint/1¼ cups single cream
1-2 garlic cloves, crushed
125 g/4 oz button mushrooms, thinly sliced
4 tbsp grated Parmesan
1-2 tbsp freshly chopped parsley

1 Poach the chicken in well-seasoned water until tender, about 10 minutes; drain and chop roughly. When cool put into a food processor with the prosciutto, spinach and onion and process until finely chopped, then add the Parmesan, allspice, seasonings and egg.

2 Roll out the pasta dough, half at a time, on a lightly floured surface until as thin as possible. Cut into 4-5 cm/ 1½-2 in rounds using a plain cutter.

3 Place ½ teaspoon of the filling in the centre of each dough circle, fold the pieces in half to make a semi-circle and press the edges firmly together. Wrap the dough semi-circle around your index finger and cross over the 2 ends, pressing firmly together, curling the rest of the dough backwards to make a "tummy button" shape. Slip the tortellini off your finger and lay on a lightly floured tray. Repeat with the rest of the dough, re-rolling the trimmings.

4 Cook the tortellini in batches: heat a large pan of salted boiling water and add some tortellini. Bring back to the boil and once they rise to the surface cook for about 5 minutes, giving an occasional stir. Remove with a slotted spoon, drain on paper towels and keep warm in a serving dish while cooking the remainder.

5 To make the sauce, heat the cream with the garlic in a pan and bring to the boil; simmer for a few minutes. Add the mushrooms, half the Parmesan and seasoning and simmer for 2-3 minutes. Stir in the parsley and pour over the warm tortellini. Sprinkle the tortellini with the remaining Parmesan and serve immediately.

SICILIAN SPAGHETTI

This delicious Sicilian dish originated as a handy way of using up leftover cooked pasta. Any variety of long pasta could be used.

SERVES 4
OVEN: 200°C/400°F/GAS 6

2 aubergines (eggplant), about 650 g/1¼ lb
150 ml/¼ pint/⅔ cup olive oil
350 g/12 oz finely minced lean beef
1 onion, peeled and chopped
2 garlic cloves, crushed
2 tbsp tomato purée (paste)
1 x 425 g/15 oz can peeled tomatoes,
     chopped
1 tsp Worcestershire sauce
1 tsp freshly chopped oregano or marjoram
     or ½ tsp dried oregano or marjoram
45 g/1½ oz pitted black olives, sliced
1 green, red or yellow (bell) pepper, cored,
     seeded and chopped
175 g/6 oz spaghetti
125 g/4 oz/1 cup grated Parmesan
salt and pepper
oregano or parsley, to garnish (optional)

1 Brush a 20 cm/8 in loose-based round cake tin with olive oil, place a disc of baking parchment in the base and oil. Trim the aubergines (eggplant) and cut into slanting slices approx 5 mm/¼ in thick. Heat some of the oil in a frying pan. Fry a few slices at a time in hot oil until lightly browned, turning once, and adding more oil as necessary. Drain on paper towels.

2 Put the minced beef, onion and garlic into a saucepan and cook, stirring frequently, until browned all over. Add the tomato purée (paste), tomatoes, Worcestershire sauce, herbs and seasoning and simmer for 10 minutes, stirring occasionally, then add the olives and (bell) pepper and continue for a further 10 minutes.

3 Heat a large pan of salted water and cook the spaghetti for 12-14 minutes until tender. Drain thoroughly. Turn the spaghetti into a bowl and mix in the meat mixture and Parmesan, combining thoroughly using two forks.

4 Lay overlapping slices of aubergine (eggplant) evenly over the base of the cake tin and up the sides. Add the meat mixture, pressing it down, and cover with the remaining slices of aubergine (eggplant).

5 Stand in a baking tin and cook in a preheated oven for 40 minutes. Leave to stand for 5 minutes then loosen around the edges and invert onto a warmed serving dish, releasing the tin clip. Remove the paper. Sprinkle with herbs before serving, if liked. Extra Parmesan cheese may be offered, if liked.

GNOCCHI ROMANA

This is a traditional recipe from Piedmont. For a less rich version, omit the eggs. It is often served as a starter before a light main course, but it makes an excellent main meal with a crisp salad.

STEP 1

SERVES 4

OVEN: 200°C/400°F, GAS 6

750 ml/ 1¼ pints/ 3 cups milk
¼ tsp grated nutmeg
90 g/ 3 oz/ 6 tbsp butter, plus extra for
  greasing
250 g/ 8 oz/ 1⅓ cups semolina
125 g/ 4 oz/ 1 cup Parmesan, finely grated
2 eggs, beaten
60 g/ 2 oz/ ½ cup Gruyère, grated
salt and pepper
basil sprigs, to garnish

1 Bring the milk to the boil, remove from the heat and stir in seasoning, nutmeg and 30 g/ 1 oz/ 2 tablespoons butter. Gradually whisk in the semolina to prevent lumps forming and return to a low heat. Simmer gently for about 10 minutes, stirring constantly, until very thick.

2 Beat 60 g/ 2 oz/ ½ cup of Parmesan into the semolina, followed by the eggs. Continue beating until it is quite smooth.

3 Spread out the semolina mixture in an even layer on a sheet of baking parchment or in a large oiled baking tin (pan), smoothing the surface with a wet spatula – it should be about 1 cm/ ½ in thick. Leave until cold, then chill for about an hour until firm.

STEP 2

4 Cut the gnocchi into circles of about 4 cm/ 1½ in, using a plain greased pastry cutter.

5 Thoroughly grease a shallow ovenproof dish, or 4 individual dishes. Lay the gnocchi trimmings in the base of the dish and cover with overlapping circles of gnocchi. Melt the remaining butter and drizzle all over the gnocchi, then sprinkle first with the remaining Parmesan and then with the grated Gruyère.

STEP 3

6 Cook in a preheated oven for 25-30 minutes until the top is crisp and golden brown.

STEP 4

NOTE

Tomato and Pepper Sauce (see page 17) may be served with this dish, if liked.

POLENTA

Polenta is prepared and served in a variety of ways and can be served hot or cold, sweet or savoury. This is the traditional way of making it in Lombardy, although there is now an instant polenta mix available.

STEP 1

SERVES 4

1.5 litres/ 2¹/₃ pints/ 7 cups water
1¹/₂ tsp salt
300 g/ 10 oz/ 2 cups polenta or cornmeal
  flour
2 beaten eggs (optional)
125 g/ 4 oz/ 2 cups fresh fine white
  breadcrumbs (optional)
vegetable oil, for frying and oiling

MUSHROOM SAUCE
250 g/ 8 oz mushrooms, sliced
3 tbsp olive oil
2 garlic cloves, crushed
150 ml/¹/₄ pint/²/₃ cup dry white wine
4 tbsp double (heavy) cream
2 tbsp freshly chopped mixed herbs
salt and pepper

1 Bring the water and salt to the boil in a large pan and gradually sprinkle in the polenta or cornmeal flour, stirring all the time to make sure the mixture is smooth and there are no lumps.

2 Simmer the mixture very gently, stirring frequently, until the polenta becomes very thick, about 30-35 minutes. It is likely to splatter, in which case partially cover the pan with a lid.

STEP 2

The mixture should become thick enough for a wooden spoon to almost stand upright in it on its own.

3 Thoroughly oil a shallow tin, about 28 x 18 cm/ 11 x 7 in, and spoon in the polenta. Spread out evenly, using a wet spatula if necessary. Leave until cold then leave for a few hours at room temperature, if possible.

4 Cut the polenta into 30-36 squares. Heat the oil in a frying pan and fry the pieces until golden brown all over, turning several times – about 5 minutes. Alternatively, dip each piece of polenta in beaten egg and coat in breadcrumbs before frying in the hot oil.

5 To make the mushroom sauce: heat the oil in a pan and fry the mushrooms with the crushed garlic for 3-4 minutes. Add the wine, season well and simmer for 5 minutes, Add the cream and chopped herbs and simmer for another minute or so.

6 Serve the polenta with the mushroom sauce. It could also be served with a tomato sauce, if preferred.

STEP 3

STEP 4

STEP 1

STEP 2

STEP 3a

STEP 3b

TAGLIATELLE WITH PUMPKIN

This unusual pasta dish comes from Emilia Romagna.

SERVES 4

500 g/ 1 lb pumpkin or butternut squash
2 tbsp olive oil
1 onion, peeled and finely chopped
2 garlic cloves, crushed
4–6 tbsp freshly chopped parsley
good pinch of ground or grated nutmeg
about 250 ml/ 8 fl oz/ 1 cup chicken or
  vegetable stock
125 g/ 4 oz Parma ham, cut into narrow
  strips
275 g/ 9 oz tagliatelle, green or white (fresh
  or dried)
150 ml/ ¼ pint/ ⅔ cup double (heavy)
  cream
salt and pepper
freshly grated Parmesan, to serve

1 Peel the pumpkin or butternut squash, removing the hard layer directly under the skin and scoop out the seeds and membrane around them. Cut the flesh into 1 cm/½ in dice.

2 Heat the oil in a pan and fry the onion and garlic gently until soft. Add half the parsley and continue for a minute or so longer.

3 Add the pumpkin or squash and continue to cook for 2-3 minutes, then season well with salt, pepper and nutmeg and add half the stock. Bring to the boil, cover and simmer for about 10 minutes or until the pumpkin is tender, adding more stock as necessary. Add the Parma ham and continue to cook for a further 2 minutes, stirring frequently.

4 Meanwhile, cook the tagliatelle in a large saucepan of boiling salted water, allowing 3-4 minutes for fresh pasta or about 12 minutes for dried (or follow the directions on the packet). When *al dente*, drain thoroughly and turn into a warmed dish.

5 Add the cream to the ham mixture and heat gently until really hot. Adjust the seasoning and spoon over the pasta. Sprinkle with the remaining parsley and hand grated Parmesan cheese separately.

FRESH PASTA

If you want to make your own pasta, use the recipe for pasta dough (see page 76), roll it out as thinly as possible and cut into narrow strips. Allow to dry on a cloth over a rack before cooking.

STEP 1

STEP 2

STEP 4

STEP 5

MILANESE RISOTTO

Italian rice is a round, short-grained variety with a nutty flavour, which is essential for a good risotto. Arborio is the very best kind to use.

SERVES 4-5

2 good pinches of saffron threads
1 large onion, finely chopped
1-2 garlic cloves, crushed
90 g/ 3 oz/ 6 tbls butter
350 g/ 12 oz 1²/₃ cups Arborio or other
  short-grain Italian rice
150 ml/¹/₄ pint/²/₃ cup dry white wine
1.25 litres/ 2 pints/ 5 cups boiling stock
  (chicken, beef or vegetable)
90 g/ 3 oz/ ³/₄ cup grated Parmesan
salt and pepper

1 Put the saffron in a small bowl, cover with 3-4 tablespoons boiling water and leave to soak while cooking the risotto.

2 Fry the onion and garlic in 60 g/ 2 oz of the butter until soft but not coloured, then add the rice and continue to cook for a few minutes until all the grains are coated in oil and beginning to colour lightly.

3 Add the wine to the rice and simmer gently, stirring from time to time until it is all absorbed.

4 Add the boiling stock a little at a time, about 150 ml/¼ pint/⅔ cup,

cooking until the liquid is fully absorbed before adding more, and stirring frequently.

5 When all the stock is absorbed the rice should be tender but not soft and soggy. Add the saffron liquid, Parmesan, remaining butter and plenty of seasoning and simmer for a minute or so until piping hot and thoroughly mixed.

6 Cover the pan tightly and leave to stand for 5 minutes off the heat. Give a good stir and serve at once.

COOKING RISOTTO

The finished dish should have moist but separate grains. This is achieved by adding the hot stock a little at a time, only adding more when the last addition is fully absorbed. Don't leave the risotto to cook by itself: it needs constant watching to see when more liquid is required.

STEP 1

STEP 2

STEP 3a

STEP 3b

CALABRIAN PIZZA

Traditionally, a Calabrian pizza has a double layer of dough to make it robust and filling. It can be made as a single pizza (as shown here). Use the second piece of dough for another base and double the filling.

SERVES 4-6
OVEN: 180°C/350°F/Gas 4

400 g/14 oz/3$\frac{1}{2}$ cups plain flour
$\frac{1}{2}$ tsp salt
1 sachet easy-blend yeast
2 tbsp olive oil
about 275 ml/9 fl oz/1 cup warm water

FILLING:
2 tbsp olive oil
2 garlic cloves , crushed
1 red (bell) pepper, cored, seeded and sliced
*1 yellow (bell) pepper, cored, seeded and
    sliced*
125 g/4 oz Ricotta
*1 x 175 g/6 oz jar sun-dried tomatoes,
    drained*
3 hard-boiled eggs, thinly sliced
1 tbsp freshly chopped mixed herbs
125 g/4 oz salami, cut into strips
150-175 g/5-6 oz Mozzarella, grated
a little milk, to glaze
salt and pepper

1 Sift the flour and salt into a bowl and mix in the easy-blend yeast then add the olive oil and enough warm water to mix to a smooth pliable dough. Knead for 10-15 minutes by hand, or process for 5 minutes in a mixer fitted with a dough hook.

2 Shape the dough into a ball, place in a lightly oiled polythene bag and put in a warm place for 1-1½ hours or until doubled in size.

3 For the filling: heat the oil in a frying pan and fry the garlic and (bell) peppers slowly in the oil until soft. Knock back the dough and roll out half to fit the base of a 30 x 25 cm/12 x 10 in oiled roasting tin. Season the dough and spread with the Ricotta, then cover with sun-dried tomatoes, hard-boiled eggs, herbs and the pepper mixture. Arrange the salami strips on top and sprinkle with the grated cheese.

4 Roll out the remaining dough and place over the filling, pressing the edges well together, or use to make a second pizza. Put to rise for about an hour in a warm place until well puffed up. An uncovered pizza will only take about 30-40 minutes to rise.

5 Prick the double pizza with a fork about 20 times, brush the top with milk and cook in a preheated oven for about 50 minutes or until lightly browned and firm to the touch. The uncovered pizza will take only 35-40 minutes. Serve hot.

Fish & Shellfish

Italians eat everything that comes out of the sea, from the smallest whitebait to the massive tuna fish, not forgetting the wide variety of shellfish. Fish markets in Italy are fascinating, with a huge variety of fish on display, but as most of their fish comes from the Mediterranean it is not always easy to find an equivalent elsewhere. However, imported frozen fish of all kinds is now appearing in fishmongers and supermarkets. After pasta, fish is probably the most important source of food in Italy, and in many recipes fish or shellfish is combined with one type of pasta or another. The inland regions of Italy such as Lombardy and Umbria have lakes with plentiful supplies of fish while Apulia has abundant supples caught by offshore trawlers. The South has splendid fish, with tuna and swordfish taking pride of place, although red mullet and sea bass are plentiful and popular too. Venice and surrounding areas have a wealth of fish and shellfish recipes, often combined with pasta, while the Ligurian coast is popular for fish soups and stews. The islands of Sicily and Sardinia abound with fish which feature widely in their cuisine, from the large tuna to the sardines which give Sardinia its name.

Opposite: The fishing fleet prepares to set off in the early morning light. Later in the day the catch – anything from John Dorey, bass, mullet, snapper and squid to lobsters and crabs – will be proudly displayed on the quayside, ready for the market.

STEP 2a

STEP 2b

STEP 4a

STEP 4b

BAKED SEA BASS

Sea bass is a delicious white-fleshed fish with a wonderful fresh flavour. If cooking 2 small fish, they can be grilled (broiled); if cooking one large fish, bake it in the oven.

SERVES 4
OVEN: 190°C/375°F/GAS 5

1.4 kg/ 3 lb fresh sea bass or 2 x 750 g/
1¹/₂ lb sea bass, gutted
2-4 sprigs fresh rosemary
¹/₂ lemon, thinly sliced
2 tbsp olive oil

GARLIC SAUCE:
2 tsp coarse sea salt
2 tsp capers
2 garlic cloves, crushed
4 tbsp water
2 fresh bay leaves
1 tsp lemon juice or wine vinegar
2 tbsp olive oil
black pepper
bay leaves and lemon wedges, to garnish

1 Scrape off the scales from the fish and cut off the sharp fins. Make diagonal cuts along both sides. Wash and dry thoroughly.

2 Place a sprig of rosemary in the cavity of each of the smaller fish with half the lemon slices; or 2 sprigs and all the lemon in the large fish. To grill (broil), place in a foil-lined pan, brush lightly with 1-2 tablespoons oil and grill (broil) under a moderate heat for about 5 minutes each side or until cooked through, turning carefully.

3 To bake: place the fish in a foil-lined dish or roasting tin brushed with oil, and brush the fish with the rest of the oil. Cook in a preheated oven for about 30 minutes for the small fish or 45-50 minutes for the large fish, until tender when tested with a skewer.

4 For the sauce: crush the salt and capers with the garlic in a pestle and mortar if available and then gradually work in the water. Alternatively, put it all into a food processor or blender and switch on until smooth. Bruise the bay leaves and remaining sprigs of rosemary and put in a bowl. Add the garlic mixture, lemon juice or vinegar and oil and pound together until the flavours are released. Season with black pepper.

5 Place the fish on a serving dish and, if liked, carefully remove the skin. Spoon some of the sauce over the fish and serve the rest separately. Garnish with fresh bay leaves and lemon wedges.

STEP 2

STEP 4

STEP 5a

STEP 5b

SARDINE AND POTATO BAKE

Fresh sardines bear very little resemblance to the canned varieties. They are now readily availalbe, frozen and sometimes fresh, so this traditional dish from Liguria can now be enjoyed by all.

SERVES 4
OVEN: 190°C/375°F/GAS 5

1 kg/2 lb potatoes, peeled
1 kg/2 lb sardines, defrosted if frozen
1 tbsp olive oil, plus extra for oiling
1 onion, peeled and chopped
2-3 garlic cloves, crushed
2 tbsp freshly chopped parsley
350 g/12 oz ripe tomatoes, peeled and sliced
    or 1 x 425 g/15 oz can peeled tomatoes,
    partly drained and chopped
1-2 tbsp freshly chopped Italian herbs (e.g.
    oregano, thyme, rosemary, marjoram)
150 ml/$^1/_4$ pint/$^2/_3$ cup dry white wine
salt and pepper

1 Put the potatoes in a pan of salted water, bring to the boil, cover and simmer for 10 minutes then drain. When cool enough to handle, cut into slices about 5 mm/¼ in thick.

2 Gut and clean the sardines: cut off their heads and tails and then slit open the length of the belly. Turn the fish over so the skin is upwards and press firmly along the backbone to loosen the bones. Turn over again and carefully remove the backbone. Wash the fish in cold water, drain well and dry them on paper towels.

3 Heat the oil in a pan and fry the onion and garlic until soft, but not coloured.

4 Arrange the potatoes in a well-oiled ovenproof dish and sprinkle with the onions and then the parsley and plenty of seasoning.

5 Lay the open sardines over the potatoes, skin-side down, then cover with the tomatoes and the rest of the herbs. Pour on the wine and season again.

6 Cook uncovered in a preheated oven for about 40 minutes until the fish is tender. If the casserole seems to be drying out, add another couple of tablespoons of wine.

V A R I A T I O N

Fresh anchovies may be used in this recipe in place of sardines. Prepare in the same way.

TROUT IN RED WINE

This recipe from Trentino is best when the fish are freshly caught, but it is a good way to cook any trout, giving it an interesting flavour.

STEP 1

STEP 3

STEP 4

STEP 5

SERVES 4

4 fresh trout, about 300 g/10 oz each
250 ml/8 fl oz/1 cup red or white wine
   vinegar
300 ml/¹/₂ pint/1¹/₄ cups red or dry white
   wine
150 ml/¹/₄ pint/²/₃ cup water
1 carrot, peeled and sliced
2-4 bay leaves
thinly pared rind of 1 lemon
1 small onion, peeled and very thinly sliced
4 sprigs fresh parsley
4 sprigs fresh thyme
1 tsp black peppercorns
6-8 whole cloves
90 g/3 oz/6 tbsp butter
1 tbsp freshly chopped mixed herbs or
   parsley
salt and pepper
herbs and lemon slices, to garnish

1 Gut the trout but leave their heads on. Dry on paper towels and lay the fish head to tail in a shallow container or baking tin just large enough to hold them.

2 Bring the wine vinegar to the boil and pour slowly all over the fish. Leave the fish to marinate for about 20 minutes.

3 Put the wine, water, carrot, bay leaves, lemon rind, onion, herbs, peppercorns and cloves into a pan with a good pinch of sea salt and heat gently.

4 Drain the fish thoroughly, discarding the vinegar. Place the fish in a fish kettle or large frying pan so they touch. When the wine mixture boils, strain gently over the fish so they are about half covered. Cover the pan and simmer very gently for 15 minutes.

5 Carefully remove the fish from the liquid, draining off as much as possible, and arrange on a serving dish.

6 Boil the cooking liquid hard until reduced to about 4-6 tablespoons. Melt the butter in a small saucepan and strain in the cooking liquor. Adjust the seasoning and spoon over the fish. Sprinkle with chopped mixed herbs and garnish with lemon and sprigs of herbs.

STEP 1a

STEP 1b

STEP 2

STEP 3

SQUID CASSEROLE

Squid and octopus are great favourites in Italy and around the Mediterranean resorts. Squid is often served fried, but here it is casseroled with tomatoes and (bell) peppers to give a rich sauce.

SERVES 4
OVEN: 180°C/350°F, GAS 4

1 kg/2 lb whole squid or 750 g/1½ lb squid
   rings, defrosted if frozen
3 tbsp olive oil
1 large onion, thinly sliced
2 garlic cloves, crushed
1 red (bell) pepper, cored, seeded and sliced
1-2 sprigs fresh rosemary
150 ml/¼ pint/⅔ cup dry white wine and
   250 ml/8 fl oz/1 cup water, or 350
   ml/12 fl oz/1½ cups water or fish stock
1 x 425 g/15 oz can peeled tomatoes,
   chopped
2 tbsp tomato purée (paste)
1 tsp paprika
salt and pepper
fresh sprigs of rosemary or parsley, to
   garnish

1 Prepare the squid (see right) and cut into 1 cm/½ in slices; cut the tentacles into lengths of about 5 cm/2 in. If using frozen squid rings, make sure they are fully defrosted and well drained.

2 Heat the oil in a flameproof casserole and fry the onion and garlic gently until soft. Add the squid rings, increase the heat and continue to cook for about 10 minutes until sealed and beginning to colour lightly. Add the red (bell) pepper, rosemary and wine (if using), and water or stock and bring up to the boil. Cover and simmer gently for 45 minutes.

3 Discard the sprigs of rosemary (but don't take out any leaves that have come off). Add the tomatoes, tomato purée (paste), seasonings and paprika. Continue to simmer gently for 45-60 minutes, or cover the casserole tightly and cook in a moderate oven for 45-60 minutes until tender.

4 Give the sauce a good stir, adjust the seasoning and serve with crusty bread.

TO PREPARE SQUID

Peel off as much as possible of the fine outer skin, using your fingers, then cut off the head and tentacles. Extract the transparent flat oval bone from the body and discard. Carefully remove the sac of black ink then turn the body sac inside out Wash thoroughly in cold water. Cut off the tentacles from the head and discard the rest; wash thoroughly.

Meat & Poultry

Italians tend to have their own special way of butchering meat, producing very different cuts. Most of their meat is sold ready boned and often cut straight across the grain. They tend to serve prime cuts and steaks very rare, so great care needs to be taken when ordering in a restaurant. Veal is a great favourite in Italy and widely available, with the popular cuts for escalopes always made straight across the grain of the meat. It is then beaten out thinly, using a meat mallet. Pork is also popular, with roast pig the traditional dish of Umbria. Suckling pig is roasted with lots of fresh herbs, especially rosemary, until the skin is crisp and brown. Lamb is often served for special occasions, cooked on a spit or roasted in the oven with wine, garlic and herbs; and the very small cutlets from young lambs feature widely, especially in Rome. Offal plays an important role in Italian cooking with liver, brains, sweetbreads, tongue, heart, tripe and kidneys always available both from veal and lamb. Poultry dishes provide some of Italy's finest food. Every part of the chicken is used, including the feet and innards for making soup. It is the spit-roasted chicken, flavoured strongly with rosemary, that has become almost a national Italian dish, being sold all over the country. Turkey, capon, duck, goose and guinea fowl are also popular, as is game. Wild rabbit and hare, wild boar and deer, are also available, especially in Sardinia.

Opposite: Italians take their food very seriously, so eating out is a very popular activity. Blessed with a wonderful climate, they can often eat outdoors, as in this Venetian restaurant.

PIZZAIOLA STEAK

This has a Neapolitan sauce, using the delicious red tomatoes so abundant in that area, but canned ones make an excellent alternative.

STEP 3

SERVES 4

*2 x 425 g/15 oz cans peeled tomatoes or
750 g/1½ lb fresh tomatoes*
4 tbsp olive oil
2-3 garlic cloves, crushed
1 onion, finely chopped
1 tbsp tomato purée (paste)
*1½ tsp freshly chopped marjoram or
oregano or ¾ tsp dried marjoram or
oregano*
2 tbsp freshly chopped parsley
1 tsp sugar
4 thin sirloin or rump steaks
salt and pepper
fresh herbs, to garnish (optional)
sauté potatoes, to serve

1 If using canned tomatoes, purée them in a food processor, then sieve to remove the seeds. If using fresh tomatoes, peel, remove the seeds and chop finely.

2 Heat half the oil in a pan and fry the garlic and onions very gently until soft – about 5 minutes.

3 Add the tomatoes, seasoning, tomato purée (paste) and chopped herbs to the pan. If using fresh tomatoes add 4 tablespoons water too, and then

STEP 4

simmer very gently for 8-10 minutes, giving an occasional stir.

4 Meanwhile, trim the steaks if necessary and season with salt and pepper. Heat the remaining oil in a frying pan and fry the steaks quickly on both sides to seal, then continue until cooked to your liking – 2 minutes for rare, 3-4 minutes for medium, or 5 minutes for well done. Alternatively, cook the steaks under a hot grill after brushing lightly with oil.

5 When the sauce has thickened a little, adjust the seasoning and stir in the chopped parsley and sugar to taste.

6 Pour off the excess fat from the pan with the steaks and add the tomato sauce. Reheat gently and serve at once, with the sauce spooned over and around the steaks. Garnish with fresh herbs, if liked. Sauté potatoes make a good accompaniment with a green vegetable.

STEP 5

ALTERNATIVE

This sauce can be served with veal and chicken. It can also be served with grilled or baked white fish.

STEP 6

STEP 1

STEP 2

STEP 3

STEP 4

VITELLO TONNATO

Veal dishes are the speciality of Lombardy, with this dish being one of the more sophisticated. Serve cold, either as part of an antipasta or as a main course. It is best served with seasonal salads.

SERVES 4

750 g/ 1 1/2 lb boned leg of veal, rolled
2 bay leaves
10 black peppercorns
2-3 whole cloves
1/2 tsp salt
2 carrots, sliced
1 onion, sliced
2 celery sticks, sliced
about 750 ml/ 1 1/4 pints / 3 cups stock or
    water
150 ml/ 1/4 pint/ 2/3 cup dry white wine
    (optional)
90 g/ 3 oz canned tuna fish, well drained
1 x 50 g (1 1/2 oz) can anchovy fillets,
    drained
150 ml/ 1/4 pint/ 2/3 cup olive oil
2 tsp bottled capers, drained
2 egg yolks
1 tbsp lemon juice
salt and pepper

TO GARNISH:
capers
lemon wedges
fresh herbs

1 Put the veal in a saucepan with the bay leaves, peppercorns, cloves, salt and vegetables. Add sufficient stock or water and the wine (if using) to barely cover the veal. Bring to the boil, remove any scum from the surface, then cover the pan and simmer gently for an hour or so until tender. Leave in the water until cold, then drain thoroughly. If time allows, chill the veal to make it easier to carve.

2 For the tuna sauce: thoroughly mash the tuna fish with 4 anchovy fillets and 1 tablespoon oil and the capers, then add the egg yolks and press through a sieve or purée in a food processor or liquidizer until smooth.

3 Stir in the lemon juice then gradually whisk in the rest of the oil a few drops at a time until the sauce is smooth and has the consistency of thick cream. Season to taste.

4 Slice the veal thinly and arrange on a flat platter in overlapping slices. Spoon the tunafish sauce over the veal to cover. Then cover the dish and chill overnight.

5 Before serving, uncover the veal carefully. Arrange the remaining anchovy fillets and the capers in a decorative pattern on top, and garnish with lemon wedges and herbs.

POT ROAST LEG OF LAMB

This dish from the Abruzzi is even better if you use a leg of mutton in place of lamb: the meat absorbs the flavours even better and becomes very tender, giving a truly memorable dish.

STEP 1

STEP 3

STEP 4

STEP 6

SERVES 4
OVEN: 180°C/350°F/ GAS 4)

1.75 kg/ 3¹/₂ lb leg of lamb
3-4 sprigs fresh rosemary
125 g/4 oz streaky bacon rashers
4 tbsp olive oil
2-3 garlic cloves, crushed
2 onions, sliced
2 carrots, sliced
2 celery sticks, sliced
300 ml/ ¹/₂ pint/ 1¹/₄ cups dry white wine
1 tbsp tomato purée (paste)
300 ml/ ¹/₂ pint/ 1¹/₄ cups stock
350 g/ 12 oz tomatoes, peeled, quartered
    and seeded
1 tbsp freshly chopped parsley
1 tbsp freshly chopped oregano or marjoram
salt and pepper
fresh rosemary sprigs, to garnish

1 Wipe the joint of lamb all over, trimming off any excess fat, then season well with salt and pepper, rubbing well in. Lay the sprigs of rosemary over the lamb, cover evenly with the bacon rashers and tie in place with fine string.

2 Heat the oil in a frying pan and fry the lamb until browned all over, turning several times – about 10 minutes. Remove from the pan.

3 Transfer the oil from the frying pan to a large fireproof casserole and fry the garlic and onion together for 3-4 minutes until beginning to soften, then add the carrots and celery and continue to cook for a few minutes longer.

4 Lay the lamb on top of the vegetables and press well to partly bury. Pour the wine over the lamb, add the tomato purée (paste) and simmer for 3-4 minutes. Add the stock, tomatoes and herbs and plenty of seasoning and bring back to the boil for a further 3-4 minutes.

5 Cover the casserole tightly and cook in a moderate oven for 2-2½ hours until very tender.

6 Remove the lamb from the casserole and if liked, take off the bacon and herbs along with the string. Keep warm. Strain the juices, skimming off any excess fat, and serve in a jug. The vegetables may be put around the joint or in a serving dish. Garnish with fresh sprigs of rosemary.

STEP 2

STEP 3

STEP 4

STEP 5

SALTIMBOCCA

Literally translated saltimbocca means "jump in the mouth", and this quick, tasty veal dish almost does that.

SERVES 4

4 thin veal escalopes
8 fresh sage leaves
4 thin slices prosciutto or Parma ham (same
  size as the veal)
flour, for dredging
2 tbsp olive oil
30 g/1 oz/2 tbsp butter
4 tbsp white wine
4 tbsp chicken stock
4 tbsp Marsala
salt and pepper
fresh sage leaves, to garnish

1 Either leave the escalopes as they are or cut in half. Place the pieces of veal on a sheet of clingfilm or baking parchment, keeping well apart, and cover with another piece.

2 Using a meat mallet or rolling pin beat the escalopes gently until at least twice their size and very thin.

3 Lightly season the veal escalopes with salt and pepper and lay 2 fresh sage leaves on the large slices, or one on each of the smaller slices. Then lay the prosciutto slices evenly over the escalopes to cover the sage and fit the size of the veal almost exactly.

4 Secure the prosciutto to the veal with wooden cocktail sticks. If preferred, the large slices can be folded in half first. Dredge lightly with a little flour.

5 Heat the olive oil and butter in a large frying pan and fry the escalopes until golden brown each side and just cooked through – about 4 minutes for single slices or 5-6 minutes for double ones. Take care not to overcook. Remove to a serving dish and keep warm.

6 Add the wine, stock and Marsala to the pan and bring to the boil, stirring well to loosen all the sediment from the pan. Boil until reduced by almost half. Adjust the seasoning and quickly pour over the saltimbocca. Serve at once, garnished with fresh sage leaves.

ALTERNATIVE

This dish can also be made using boneless chicken breasts. Slit the breasts almost in half, open out and beat as thinly as possible, as for the veal.

CHICKEN WITH GREEN OLIVES

Olives are a popular flavouring for poultry and game in Apulia, where this recipe originates. In Italy every morsel of the bird is used in some way, most often for soups and stock.

STEP 1

SERVES 4

OVEN: 180°C/350°F/ GAS 4

4 chicken breasts, part boned
30 g/1 oz/2 tbsp butter
2 tbsp olive oil
1 large onion, finely chopped
2 garlic cloves, crushed
2 (bell) peppers, red, yellow or green, cored, seeded and cut into large pieces
250 g/8 oz large closed cup mushrooms, sliced or quartered
175 g/6 oz tomatoes, peeled and halved
150 ml/¹/₄ pint/²/₃ cup dry white wine
125-175 g/4-6 oz green olives, pitted
4-6 tbsp double (heavy) cream
salt and pepper
flat-leaf parsley, chopped, to garnish

1 Season the chicken with salt and pepper. Heat the oil and butter in a frying pan, add the chicken and fry until browned all over. Remove from the pan.

2 Add the onion and garlic to the pan and fry gently until beginning to soften. Add the (bell) peppers to the pan with the mushrooms and continue to cook for a few minutes longer.

3 Add the tomatoes and plenty of seasoning to the pan and then

STEP 2

transfer the vegetable mixture to an ovenproof casserole. Place the chicken on the bed of vegetables.

4 Add the wine to the frying pan and bring to the boil. Pour the wine over the chicken and cover the casserole tightly. Cook in a preheated oven for 50 minutes.

5 Add the olives to the chicken, mix lightly then pour on the cream. Re-cover the casserole and return to the oven for 10-20 minutes or until the chicken is very tender.

6 Adjust the seasoning and serve the pieces of chicken, surrounded by the vegetables and sauce, with pasta or tiny new potatoes. Sprinkle with parsley to garnish.

STEP 3

NOODLES

Serve this dish with freshly made ribbon noodles for a really attractive presentation. Fresh pasta takes only 2-3 minutes to cook.

STEP 5

LIVER WITH WINE SAUCE

Liver is popular in Italy and is served in many ways. The ideal is calf's liver, but this is expensive and not always readily available, so use lamb's liver as an alternative.

STEP 1

SERVES 4

4 slices calf's liver or 8 slices lamb's liver,
   about 500 g/1 lb
flour, for coating
1 tbsp olive oil
30 g/1 oz/2 tbls butter
1garlic clove, crushed
125 g/4 oz lean bacon rashers, rinded
1 onion, chopped
1 celery stick, thinly sliced
150 ml/¹/₄ pint/²/₃ cup red wine
150 ml/¹/₄ pint/²/₃ cup beef stock
good pinch of ground allspice
1 tsp Worcestershire sauce
1 tsp freshly chopped sage or ¹/₂ tsp
   dried sage
3-4 tomatoes, peeled
salt and pepper
fresh sage leaves, to garnish
sauté potatoes, to serve

1 Wipe the liver, season with salt and pepper and coat lightly in flour, shaking off the surplus.

2 Heat the oil and butter in a pan and fry the liver until well sealed on both sides and just cooked through – take care not to overcook. Remove the liver from the pan, cover and keep warm, but do not allow to dry out.

3 Cut the bacon into narrow strips and add to the fat left in the pan with the onion and celery. Fry gently until soft.

4 Add the wine and stock, allspice, Worcestershire sauce and seasonings, bring to the boil and simmer for 3-4 minutes.

5 Quarter the tomatoes, discard the seeds and cut each piece in half. Add to the sauce and continue to cook for a couple of minutes.

6 Serve the liver on a little of the sauce, with the remainder spooned over. Garnish with fresh sage leaves and serve with tiny new potatoes or sauté potatoes.

STEP 2

STEP 3

COOKING LIVER

Overcooked liver is dry and tasteless, especially when it is coated in flour. Cook the slices for only 2-3 minutes on each side – they should be soft and tender, and still a little pink in the centre.

STEP 4

Desserts

Many Italians prefer to finish their meal with a bowl of mixed fruits or fruits with cheese, but they do like their desserts too. When there is a family gathering or a celebration, then a special effort is made and the delicacies appear. The Sicilians are said to have the sweetest tooth of all, and many Italian desserts are thought to have originated there. Ice-creams (gelato), sorbets and water ices (granita) are said to be borrowed from the Arabs, who occupied their island centuries ago, and you have to go a very long way to beat a Sicilian ice-cream, especially the famous cassata and ricotta ice-creams. Fruits feature in desserts too. The famous pear tarts of the north are mouthwatering, using the very best fruit blended with apricot jam, sultanas and almonds, while oranges appear marinated in syrup and liqueur. Biscuits with almond flavouring are often served as an accompaniment, and the famous florentines – biscuits full of glacé fruit and covered with chocolate – are favourites too. Gâteaux are popular, often incorporating mascarpone or ricotta cheese along with citrus fruits and honey. Tiramisu is a favourite with all, and for Christmas and special occasions try the honey cake from Siena called Panforte – so very rich that even a tiny piece will leave you with delicious memories for a very long time.

Opposite: *The fertile plains of Tuscany grow an enormous variety of fruit and vegetables. Many famous desserts originate here, including the luscious Panforte di Siena*

STEP 1a

STEP 1b

STEP 2

STEP 5

TIRAMISU

A favourite Italian dessert which is found in many regions. Here it is flavoured with coffee and Amaretto, but you could also use Marsala and Maraschino.

SERVES 4-6

20-24 sponge fingers (boudoir biscuits),
    about 150 g/5 oz
2 tbsp cold black coffee
2 tbsp coffee essence
2 tbsp Amaretto or brandy
4 egg yolks (size 2 or 3)
90 g/3 oz/6 tbsp caster sugar
few dropsof vanilla essence
grated rind of ½ lemon
350 g/12 oz/1½cups Mascarpone (Italian
    full-fat cream cheese)
2 tsp lemon juice
250 ml/8 fl oz/1 cup double(heavy) cream
1 tbsp milk
30 g/1 oz/¼ cup flaked almonds, lightly
    toasted
2 tbsp cocoa powder
1 tbsp icing (confectioner's) sugar

1 Arrange almost half the sponge fingers in the base of a glass bowl or serving dish. Combine the black coffee, coffee essence and Amaretto or brandy and sprinkle just over half the mixture over the fingers.

2 Put the egg yolks into a heatproof bowl with the sugar, vanilla essence and lemon rind. Stand over a saucepan of gently simmering water and whisk until very thick and creamy and the whisk leaves a very heavy trail when lifted from the bowl.

3 Put the Mascarpone cheese into a bowl, add the lemon juice and beat until smooth.

4 Combine the egg mixture and Mascarpone cheese and when evenly blended pour half over the sponge fingers and spread out evenly.

5 Add another layer of sponge fingers, sprinkle with the remaining coffee and then cover with the rest of the cheese mixture. Chill for at least 2 hours and preferably longer, or overnight.

6 To serve, whip the cream and milk together until fairly stiff and spread or pipe over the dessert. Sprinkle with the flaked almonds and then sift an even layer of cocoa powder so the top is completely covered. Finally sift a very light layer of icing sugar over the cocoa.

ZABAGLIONE

This light, sweet dessert is reminiscent of a whisked egg custard. Serve warm or chilled, accompanied by sponge fingers or amaretti biscuits, and soft fruits such as strawberries or raspberries.

STEP 1

SERVES 4

6 egg yolks
90 g / 3 oz / 6 tbsp caster sugar
6 tbsp Marsala
amaretti biscuits or sponge fingers, to serve
strawberries or raspberries, to decorate
   (optional)

1 Put the egg yolks into a heatproof bowl and whisk until a pale yellow colour, using a rotary, balloon or electric whisk.

2 Whisk in the sugar, followed by the Marsala, continuing to whisk all the time.

3 Stand the bowl over a saucepan of very gently simmering water, or transfer to the top of a double boiler, and continue to whisk continuously. Whisk until the mixture thickens sufficiently to stand in soft peaks. On no account allow the water to boil or the zabaglione will over-cook and turn into scrambled eggs.

4 Scrape around the sides of the bowl from time to time while whisking. As soon as the mixture is really thick and foamy, take from the heat and continue to whisk for a couple of minutes longer.

STEP 2

5 Pour immediately into stemmed glasses and serve warm; or leave until cold and serve chilled.

6 Fruits such as strawberries or raspberries or crumbled sponge fingers or amaretti biscuits may be placed in the base of the glasses before adding the zabaglione.

STEP 3

ALTERNATIVE

Any other type of liqueur may be used in place of Marsala, for a change.

STEP 4

STEP 1

STEP 2

STEP 3

STEP 5

PANFORTE DI SIENA

This famous Tuscan honey and nut cake is a Christmas speciality. In Italy it is sold in pretty boxes, which seems to make it taste even better. Panforte is very rich and sticky and should be served in very thin slices.

SERVES 12
OVEN: 150°C/300°F/ GAS 2

125 g/4 oz/1 cup split whole almonds
125 g/4 oz/³⁄₄ cup hazelnuts
90 g/3 oz/¹⁄₂ cup cut mixed peel
60 g/2 oz/¹⁄₃ cup no-need-to-soak dried
   apricots
60 g/2 oz glacé or crystallized pineapple
grated rind of 1 large orange
60 g/2 oz/¹⁄₂ cup plain flour
2 tbsp cocoa powder
2 tsp ground cinnamon
125 g/4 oz/¹⁄₂ cup caster sugar
175 g/6 oz/¹⁄₂ cup honey
icing (confectioner's) sugar, for dredging

1 Toast the almonds until lightly browned and place in a bowl. Toast the hazelnuts under the grill until the skins split. Place the hazelnuts on a tea towel and rub off the skins with the towel. Roughly chop the hazelnuts and add to the almonds with the mixed peel.

2 Chop the apricots and pineapple fairly finely, add to the nuts with the orange rind and mix well.

3 Sift the flour with the cocoa and cinnamon, add to the nut mixture and mix evenly.

4 Line a round 20 cm/8 in cake tin or deep loose-based flan tin with baking parchment.

5 Put the sugar and honey into a saucepan and heat until the sugar dissolves, then boil gently for about 5 minutes or until the mixture thickens and begins to turn a deeper shade of brown. Quickly add to the nut mixture and stir through it evenly. Turn into the prepared tin and level the top with the help of a damp spoon.

6 Cook in a cool oven for an hour. Remove from the oven and leave in the tin until cold. Take out of the tin and carefully peel off the paper. Before serving, dredge the cake heavily with sifted icing (confectioner's) sugar. Serve cut into very thin slices.

STORAGE

Panforte will keep for several weeks stored in an airtight container or securely wrapped in foil.

PEAR TART

Pears are a very popular fruit in Italy. In this recipe from Trentino they are flavoured with almonds, cinnamon, raisins and apricot jam, then baked in an open tart with a soft-textured sweet pastry.

STEP 1

SERVES 4-6
OVEN: 200°C/400°F/GAS 6

275 g/9 oz/2¼ cups plain flour
pinch of salt
125 g/4 oz/½ cup caster sugar
125 g/4 oz/½ cup butter, diced
1 egg
1 egg yolk
few drops of vanilla essence
2-3 tsp water

FILLING:
4 tbsp apricot jam
60 g/2 oz amaretti or ratafia biscuits, crumbled
850-1 kg/1¾-2 lb pears, peeled and cored
1 tsp ground cinnamon
90 g/3 oz/½ cup raisins or sultanas
60 g/2 oz/⅓ cup soft brown or demerara sugar
sifted icing (confectioner's) sugar, for sprinkling

1 Sift the flour and salt onto a flat surface, make a well in the centre and add the sugar, butter, egg, egg yolk, vanilla essence and most of the water.

2 Using your fingers gradually work the flour into the other ingredients to give a smooth, pliable dough, adding a little more water, if necessary. Wrap in clingfilm and chill for an hour or until firm. Alternatively, put all the ingredients into a food processor and process until evenly blended and smooth.

STEP 3

3 Using almost ¾ of the dough, roll it out and use to line a shallow 25 cm/10 in cake tin or deep flan tin. Spread the apricot jam over the base and sprinkle with the crushed biscuits.

4 Slice the pears very thinly. Arrange the pear slices over the biscuits in the pastry case. Sprinkle first with cinnamon then with raisins, and finally with the brown sugar.

STEP 4

5 Roll out a thin sausage shape using about ⅛ of the remaining dough, and place around the edge of the pie. Roll the remainder into thin sausages and arrange in a lattice over the pie, 4 or 5 strips in each direction, attaching to the strip around the edge.

6 Cook in a preheated oven for about 50 minutes until golden brown and cooked through. Remove from the oven and leave to cool. Serve warm or chilled, sprinkled with sifted icing (confectioner's) sugar.

STEP 5

CARAMELIZED ORANGE

The secret of these oranges is to allow them to marinate in the syrup for at least 24 hours, and preferably longer, so the caramel and liqueur can penetrate to the centre of the fruit.

STEP 3

SERVES 6

6 large oranges
250 g/8 oz/1 cup caster or granulated sugar
250 ml/8 fl oz/1 cup water
6 whole cloves (optional)
2-4 tbsp Grand Marnier, Curaçao or brandy

1 Use a citrus zester or potato peeler to pare off the rind from 2 oranges, to give narrow strips of peel without any of the white pith attached. If using a potato peeler cut into very thin julienne strips using a very sharp knife.

2 Put the strips into a small saucepan and barely cover with water. Bring to the boil and simmer for 5 minutes until tender. Drain the strips and reserve the water.

3 Cut away all the white pith and peel from the oranges using a very sharp knife and then cut horizontally into 4 slices. Reassemble the oranges and hold in place with wooden cocktail sticks. Stand in a heatproof dish.

4 Put the sugar and water into a heavy-based saucepan with the cloves, if using. Bring to the boil and simmer gently until the sugar has

dissolved, then boil hard without stirring until the syrup thickens and begins to turn brown. Continue to cook until a light golden brown then quickly remove from the heat and carefully pour in the reserved liquor from cooking the orange rind.

5 Return to a gentle heat until the caramel has fully dissolved again, then remove from the heat, add the liqueur or brandy and when mixed pour over the oranges.

6 Sprinkle the orange strips over the oranges, cover with clingfilm and leave until cold. Chill for at least 3 hours and preferably for 24-48 hours before serving. If time allows, spoon the syrup over the oranges several times whilst they are marinating. Discard the cocktail stick before serving.

STEP 4

STEP 5

CARAMEL

To make caramel the sugar syrup is boiled until it turns golden brown and reaches the "small crack" stage, 138-152°C/280-305°F on a sugar thermometer.

STEP 6

RICOTTA ICE-CREAM

Ice-cream is one of the traditional dishes of Italy. Everyone eats it and there are "gelato" stalls abounding which sell numerous flavours, usually in a cone. It is also served sliced, as in this classic from Sicily.

STEP 1

STEP 2

STEP 4

STEP 5

SERVES 4-6

30 g/ 1 oz/¹/₄ cup pistachio nuts
30 g/ 1 oz/¹/₄ cup walnuts or pecan nuts
30 g/ 1 oz/¹/₄ cup toasted chopped hazelnuts
grated rind of 1 orange
grated rind of 1 lemon
30 g/ 1 oz/ 2 tbsp crystallized or stem ginger
30 g/ 1 oz/ 2 tbsp glacé cherries
30 g/ 1 oz/¹/₄ cup no-need-to-soak dried apricots
30 g/ 1 oz/ 3tbsp raisins
500 g/ 1 lb/ 1¹/₂ cups Ricotta
2 tbsp Maraschino, Amaretto or brandy
1 tsp vanilla essence
4 egg yolks
125 g/ 4 oz/¹/₂ cup caster sugar

TO DECORATE:
whipped cream
few glacé cherries, pistachio nuts or mint leaves

1 Roughly chop the pistachio nuts and walnuts and mix with the toasted hazelnuts, orange and lemon rind. Finely chop the ginger, cherries, apricots and raisins and add to the bowl.

2 Mix the ricotta evenly through the fruit mixture then beat in the liqueur and essence.

3 Put the egg yolks and sugar in a bowl and whisk hard until very thick and creamy – they may be whisked over a pan of gently simmering water to speed up the process. Leave to cool, if necessary.

4 Carefully fold the ricotta mixture evenly through the beaten eggs and sugar until smooth.

5 Line a 18 x 12 cm/ 7 x 5 in loaf tin (pan) with a double layer of clingfilm or baking parchment, pour in the ricotta mixture, level the top, cover with more clingfilm or baking parchment and chill in the freezer until firm – at least overnight.

6 To serve, carefully remove the ice-cream from the tin (pan) and peel off the paper. Stand on a serving dish and if liked decorate with whipped cream using a piping bag and star vegetable nozzle, and glacé cherries and/or pistachio nuts. Serve in slices, with mint leaves, if liked.

ITALIAN FOOD BY REGION

PASTA DOUGH

*325 g/11 oz/generous 2¹/₂ cups
    plain flour
3 large eggs
1 tbsp olive oil
1 tbsp water
salt*

1. To make the pasta dough,
sift the flour and a pinch of salt
onto a flat surface and make a
well in the centre.

2. Beat the eggs, oil and water
together and gradually pour
this liquid into the centre of the
flour, working in the flour with
your hand, a little at a time
until it all comes together to
make a dough.

3. Knead for about 5 minutes
until smooth. Cover with a
damp cloth or put into a lightly
oiled polythene bag and leave
to rest for 5-15 minutes.

There are two main culinary zones in
Italy: the wine and olive zone, which lies
around Umbria, Liguria and the South;
and the cattle country, where the olive
tree will not flourish – Emilia-Romagna,
Lombardy and Veneto – but where milk
and butter are widely produced. Tuscany
uses both butter and oil in its cooking
because cattle flourish in the area and so
do the olive trees.

PIEDMONT
The name means "at the foot of the
mountain", which it is, bordering on
both France and Switzerland. Its fertile
arable fields are irrigated by the many
canals which flow through the region.

The food is substantial, peasant-type
fare, though the fragrant white truffle is
found in this region. Truffles can be
finely flaked or grated and added to
many of the smarter dishes, but they are
wildly expensive. There is also an
abundance of wild mushrooms
throughout the region. Garlic features
strongly in the recipes and polenta,
gnocchi and rice are eaten in larger
quantities than pasta, the former offered
as a first course when soup is not served.
A large variety of game is also widely
available in the area.

LOMBARDY
The mention of the capital, Milan,
produces immediate thoughts of the
wonderful risotto named after the city
and also the Milanese soufflé flavoured
strongly with lemon. Veal dishes,

including *vitello tonnato* and *osso buco*,
are specialties of the region and other
excellent meat dishes, particularly pot
roasts, feature widely.

The lakes of the area produce a wealth
of fresh fish. Rice and polenta are again
popular but pasta also appears in many
guises. The famous sweet yeasted cake
Panettone is a product of this region.

TRENTINO-ALTO-ADIGE
This is a double area with a strong
Germanic influence, particularly when it
comes to the wines. There are also
several liqueurs produced, still with a
German influence, such as Aquavit,
Kümmel and Slivovitz.

The foods are robust and basic in this
mountainous area with rich green
valleys and lakes where fish are plentiful.
In the Trentino area particularly, pasta
and simple meat and offal dishes are
popular, while in the Adige soups and
pot roasts are favoured, often with added
dumplings and spiced sausages.

VENETO
The cooking in this north-east corner is
straightforward, with abundant servings
of polenta with almost everything. The
land is intensely farmed, providing
mostly cereals and wine. Pasta is more in
the background with polenta, gnocchi
and rice more favoured. Fish,
particularly seafood, is in abundance
and especially good seafood salads are
widely available. There are also excellent
robust soups and risottos flavoured with

the seafood and sausages of the area.

LIGURIA

The Genoese are excellent cooks, and all along the Italian Riviera coast can be found fantastic trattoria which produce amazing fish dishes flavoured with the local olive oil. Pesto sauce flavoured with basil, cheese and pine kernels comes from this area, along with other excellent sauces. The aroma of fresh herbs abounds, widely used in many dishes, including their famous pizzas.

EMILIA-ROMAGNA

This is a special region of high gastronomic importance, with an abundance of everything, and rich food is widely served. Tortellini and lasagne feature widely, along with many other pasta dishes, as do saltimbocca and other veal dishes. Parma is famous for its ham, *prosciutto di Parma*, thought to be the best in the world. Balsamic vinegar, which has grown in popularity over the past decade, is also produced here, from wine which is distilled until it is dark brown and extremely strongly flavoured.

TUSCANY

The Tuscans share a great pride in cooking and eating with the Emilians, and are known to have hefty appetites. Tuscany has everything: an excellent coastal area providing splendid fish, and hills covered in vineyards and fertile plains where every conceivable vegetable and fruit happily grows. There is plenty of game in the region, providing many interesting recipes; tripe cooked in a thick tomato sauce is popular along with many liver recipes; beans in many

guises appear frequently, as well as pot roasts, steaks and full-bodied soups, all of which are well favoured.

Florence has a wide variety of specialties, while Siena boasts the famous candied fruit cake called Panforte di Siena.

UMBRIA/MARCHES

Inland Umbria is famous for its pork, and the character of the cuisine is marked by the use of the local fresh ingredients, including lamb, game and fish from the lakes, but is not spectacular on the whole. Spit-roasting and grilling is popular, and the excellent local olive oil is used both in cooking and to pour over dishes before serving. Black truffles, olives, fruit and herbs are plentiful and feature in many recipes. Eastwards to the Marches the wealth of fish from the coast adds even more to the variety and the food tends to be more on the elaborate side, with almost every restaurant noted for its excellent cuisine. First-class sausages and cured pork come from the Marches, particularly on the Umbrian border, and pasta features widely all over the region.

LAZIO

Rome is the capital of both Lazio and Italy and thus has become a focal point for specialities from all over Italy. Food from this region tends to be fairly simple and quick to prepare, hence the many pasta dishes with delicious sauces, gnocchi in various forms and plenty of dishes featuring lamb and veal (saltimbocca being just one), and offal, all with plenty of herbs and seasonings

COOKING PASTA

Pasta comes in all shapes and sizes and is available both fresh and dried. It is often said that the larger the pasta shapes, the richer the sauce should be, but that is a matter of preference: you can serve your favourite sauce with your favourite pasta, whatever the shape or what anyone says – the main thing is to enjoy it.

It is also said that guests should wait for the pasta to be ready and not vice versa; but as pasta does not take long to cook that should not present a problem. Always make sure it is served *al dente*, i.e. tender but still with a slight bite to it – soggy pasta is not very palatable, at least not to Italians and true lovers of pasta!

Allow 90-125 g/3-4 oz pasta per head for a main dish and add to a pan of lightly salted gently simmering water, with a teaspoon of oil to help keep the pasta separate. Never fully cover the pan: either partly cover or leave totally uncovered, and once it has come back to the boil, give a good stir, then turn the heat down and simmer for about 5 minutes for tiny pasta, 8-10 minutes for medium pasta and 10-15 minutes for large shapes. Fresh pasta of all types only takes a few minutes to cook. Always drain thoroughly before serving, and serve hot. For a salad, it may be rinsed under cold water to cool it down rapidly.

MAIN PASTA VARIETIES

Lasagne Everyone knows the flat pasta sheets, either plain or ridged, in plain egg, spinach and wholewheat varieties. Nowadays dried lasagne rarely needs pre-cooking, which speeds up the whole process. Simply layer with a fairly runny meat, fish or vegetable mixture together with a cheese or white sauce and brown in the oven.

Canneloni Large tubes which are usually stuffed with a meat, fish or vegetable mixture and cooked in a cheesey sauce or strong garlic and tomato sauce. Canneloni can also be made by rolling up cooked sheets of lasagne around the filling.

Penne Shaped like quills with slanting ends and approx 2.5-4 cm/1-1½ in long, they are always smooth tubes.

Tortellini Pasta pockets shaped into curls. Often filled with a savoury meat, fish , cheese or vegetable forcemeat.

Spaghetti The best known type of pasta, available anywhere and everywhere.

Tagliatelle Narrow pasta strips, usually shaped into nests when sold dried in packets. Available in egg, spinach, wholewheat and tomato flavours.

giving really robust flavours and delicious sauces. Vegetables feature along with the fantastic fruits which are always in abundance in the local markets; and beans appear both in soups and many other dishes. The main theme of this region is strongly flavoured food with robust sauces.

ABRUZZI AND MOLISE

Another divided region with an interior of mountains with river valleys, high plateaux, densely forested areas and a coastal plain. The cuisine here is deeply traditional, with local hams and cheeses from the mountain areas, interesting sausages with plenty of garlic and other seasonings, cured meats, wonderful fish and seafood, which is the main produce of the coastal areas, where fishing boats abound on the beaches. Lamb features widely: tender, juicy and well-flavoured with herbs.

CAMPANIA

Naples is the home of pasta dishes, served with a splendid tomato sauce (with many variations) whose fame has spread worldwide. Pizza is said to have been created in Naples and now has spread to the north of the country and indeed worldwide.

Fish abounds, with *fritto misto* and *fritto pesce* being great favourites, varying daily depending on the catch. Fish stews are robust and varied and shellfish in particular is often served with pasta. Cutlets and steaks are excellent, served with strong sauces usually flavoured with garlic, tomatoes and herbs: pizzaiola steak is one of the favourites. Excellent

Mozzarella cheese is produced locally and used to create the crispy Mozarella in Carozza, again served with a garlicky tomato sauce. Sweet dishes are popular too, often with flaky pastry and Ricotta cheese, and the seasonal fruit salads laced with wine or liqueur take a lot of beating.

PUGLIA (APULIA)

The ground is stony but it produces good fruit, olive groves, vegetables and herbs, and, of course, there is a large amount of seafood from the sea. Puglians are said to be champion pasta eaters: many of the excellent pasta dishes are exclusive to the region both in shape and ingredients. Mushrooms abound and are always added to the local pizzas.

Oysters and mussels are plentiful, and so is octopus. Brindisi is famous for its shellfish – both the seafood salads and risottos are truly memorable. But it is not all fish or pasta: lamb is roasted and stewed to perfection and so is veal, always with plenty of herbs.

BASILICATA

This is a sheep-farming area, mainly mountainous, where potent wines are produced to accompany a robust cuisine largely based on pasta, lamb, pork, game and abundant dairy produce. The salamis and cured meats are excellent, as are the mountain hams. Lamb is flavoured from the herbs and grasses on which it feeds. Wonderful thick soups – true minestrone – are produced in the mountains, and eels and fish are plentiful in the lakes. Chilli peppers are grown in this region and appear in many of the recipes. They are not overpoweringly strong, although the flavours of the region in general tend to be quite strong and intense. The cheeses are excellent, with good fruits grown and interesting local bread baked in huge loaves.

CALABRIA

This is the toe of Italy, where orange and lemon groves flourish along with olive groves and a profusion of vegetables, especially aubergines (eggplant) which are cooked in a variety of ways.

Chicken, rabbit and guinea fowl are often on the menu. Pizzas feature largely, often with a fishy topping. Mushrooms grow well in the Calabrian climate and feature in many dishes from sauces and stews to salads. Pasta comes with a great variety of sauces including baby artichokes, eggs, meat, cheese, mixed vegetables, the large sweet (bell) peppers of the region and of course garlic. The fish is excellent too and here fresh tunafish and swordfish are available with many other varieties.

Like most southern Italians, the Calabrians are sweet-toothed and many desserts and cakes are flavoured with aniseed, honey and almonds and featuring the plentiful figs of the region.

SICILY

This is the largest island in the Mediterranean and the cuisine is largely based on fish and vegetables. Fish soups, stews and salads appear in unlimited forms, including tuna, swordfish, mussels and many more; citrus fruits are widely grown along with almonds and pistachio nuts, and the local wines, including Marsala, are excellent.

Meat is often given a long, slow cooking, or else is minced and shaped before cooking. Game is plentiful and is often cooked in sweet-sour sauces containing the local black olives.

Pasta abounds again with more unusual sauces as well as the old favourites. All Sicilians have a love of desserts, cakes and especially ice-cream. Cassata and other ice-creams from Sicily are famous all over the world, and the huge variety of flavours of both cream ices and granita makes it difficult to decide which is your favourite.

SARDINIA

A pretty island with a wealth of flowers in the spring, but the landscape dries out in the summer from the hot sun. The national dish is suckling pig. or newborn lamb cooked on an open fire or spit; and rabbit, game and offal dishes are very popular.

The sweet dishes are numerous and often extremely delicate, and for non-sweet eaters there is fresh fruit of almost every kind in abundance.

Fish is top quality, with excellent sea bass, lobsters, tuna, mullet, eels and mussels in good supply.

The island has a haunting aroma which drifts from many kitchens – it is myrtle (*mirto*), a local herb which is added to anything and everything from chicken to the local liqueur; and along with the wonderful cakes and breads of Sardinia, myrtle will long remain a memory of the island when you have returned home.

Fettucine These are medium wide pasta strips with wavy edges, ideal to serve with meat and shellfish sauces.

Rigatoni Similar to penne but shorter and with a ridged surface.

Fusilli Also called spirals because they resemble corkscrews.They come in all colours and flavours including wholewheat, often mixed together in packets. Also excellent in salads.

Farfalle These are bows of medium size, again made in all flavours of pasta to serve in a wide variety of hot dishes as well as salads.

Ravioli Square parcels of pasta with a spicy meat filling, cut with a shaped pasta cutter to give wavy edges, then poached and served in a variety of sauces.

Macaroni A fairly thick, tubular pasta available in different lengths and thicknesses. Some are almost straight while others are curved, and called "elbow" macaroni. Ideal to serve with any type of sauce and also great in salad.

INDEX